SOTHEBY, WILKINSON & HODGE.

WELLINGTON STREET, STRAND.

# CATALOGUE

OF

## A VALUABLE COLLECTION

OF CHOICE

# GREEK & ROMAN COINS,

## In Gold and Silver,

*Received from Constantinople.*

### Days of Sale.

FIRST DAY ...... Friday, 23rd June ............ LOTS    1 to 159
SECOND DAY ... Saturday, 24th June ......... LOTS 160 to 356

## 1882.

# CATALOGUE

OF

## A VALUABLE COLLECTION

OF CHOICE

# GREEK & ROMAN COINS,

In Gold and Silver,

## RECEIVED FROM CONSTANTINOPLE,

INCLUDING

### AMONGST NUMEROUS RARITIES

Camarina, Selinus, Timotheus and Dionysius, Mausolus, Nagidus, Mallus, Shekels, numerous Tetradrachms of Syria: Sanä, Ariarathes IV, Volarsaces, Tripolis, Arsinoe, Berenice, Ptolemy I (*gold*, with Quadriga of Elephants).

Julius Cæsar, Antonia, Plotina, Matidia, Crispina, &c., including many Byzantine:

ALSO

## Some good small Coin Cabinets in Mahogany,

&c. &c.

## WHICH WILL BE SOLD BY AUCTION,

BY MESSRS.

# SOTHEBY, WILKINSON & HODGE,

Auctioneers of Literary Property & Works illustrative of the Fine Arts.

AT THEIR HOUSE, No. 13, WELLINGTON STREET, STRAND. W.C.

On FRIDAY, the 23rd day of JUNE. 1882. and following Day,

AT ONE O'CLOCK PRECISELY.

May be Viewed Two Days previously, and Catalogues had.

DRYDEN PRESS: J. Davy and Sons, 137, Long Acre.

# CONDITIONS OF SALE.

I. The highest bidder to be the buyer; and if any dispute arise between bidders, the lot so disputed shall be immediately put up again, provided the auctioneer cannot decide the said dispute.

II. No person to advance less than 1s.; above five pounds, 2s. 6d., and so on in proportion.

III. In the case of lots upon which there is a reserve, the auctioneer shall have the right to bid on behalf of the seller.

IV. The purchasers to give in their names and places of abode, and to pay down 5s. in the pound, if required, in part payment of the purchase-money; in default of which the lot or lots purchased to be immediately put up again and re-sold.

V. The Sale of any lot is not to be set aside on account of any error in the enumeration of the numbers stated, or errors of description.

VI. The lots to be taken away, at the buyer's expense, immediately after the conclusion of the sale; in default of which Messrs. SOTHEBY, WILKINSON, and HODGE will not hold themselves responsible if lost, stolen, damaged, or otherwise destroyed, but they will be left at the sole risk of the purchaser. If, at the expiration of Two Days after the conclusion of the sale, the lots are not cleared or paid for, they will then be catalogued for immediate sale, and the expense, the same as if re-sold, will be added to the amount at which they were bought. Messrs. SOTHEBY, WILKINSON and HODGE will have the option of re-selling the lots uncleared either by public or private sale, without any notice being given to the defaulter.

VII. Upon failure of complying with the above conditions, the money required and deposited in part of payment shall be forfeited, and *if any loss is sustained in the re-selling of such lots as are not cleared or paid for, all charges on such re-sale shall be made good by the defaulters at this sale.*

---

*Gentlemen who cannot attend this Sale, may have their Commissions faithfully executed by their humble Servants.*

SOTHEBY, WILKINSON & HODGE.

13, Wellington Street. Strand.

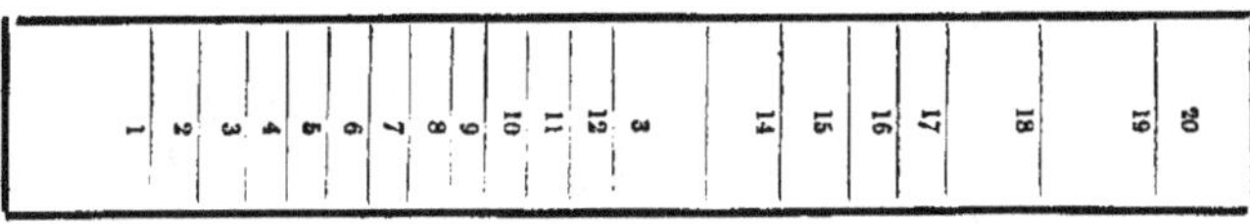

Sizes of the Coins. Scale of Mionnet.

# CATALOGUE

OF

### A COLLECTION OF VALUABLE

# GREEK AND ROMAN COINS,

*FROM CONSTANTINOPLE.*

## FIRST DAY'S SALE.

### GREEK COINS IN SILVER.

LOT

*Lincoln* 1 Massalia Galliae, Æ, head of Apollo, *rev.* Circle divided into quadrants, in two of which MA.    *size* 1.  22    *16*

*Do.* 2 Others    18    *13*

*Bunbury* 3 Populonia in Etruria, *obv.* bearded Head, *rev.* plain, about 600 B.C.    *size* 5.  1    *1 1*

  **** The silver money of this place is especially remarkable for being generally of a pecular fabric, in which the reverse is left perfectly plain.

*Mason* 4 Samnium, Social or Marsic War Denarius, *obv.* ITALIA. *rev.* Eight Confederates, &c.    1    *10*

*Do.* 5 Another, Oscan legends, four Chiefs, &c.    1    *10*

*Bunbury* 6 Another, two Chiefs, &c. as on Consular Coins of the Veturii    1    *1 12*

*Dodgson* 7 Atella Campaniæ, Æ, Triens, *rev.* Quadriga to right, ATERL. in Samnite characters    *size* 9.  1    *2-*

*Jennings* 8 Capua, Æ, *rev.* Eagle to right, *rare*    *size* 10.  1    *3*

9 Cales, Æ, Head of Pallas to right, behind, spear's head, *rev.* Biga to left, and CALENO. *didrachm*    1    *3*

B

10 Cumea; Diademate Head of the Syren Parthenope to right,
rev. KVMAION, oyster shell, star above, all in dotted
circle, *rare*                          *size* 4½.   1

11 Nuceria-Alaphaterna with complete Oscan legend, dolphin
behind the Head of Sarnus, *rev.* heroic Figure holds
horse to left, *a gem*                    *size* 5.   1

12 Hyrina, *rev.* YDINA (Archaic, retrograde) Andromorphous
Bull to left                              *size* 5.   1

13 Phistelia, full-faced Head of Apollo, *rev.* Bull to left, dolphin
as exergum, *a fine didrachm or hemi-stater*         1

14 Tarentum. Taras the son of Neptune to left with trident, diota,
AP. and dolphin, *rev.* naked victorious Horseman to right,
with spear, buckler and two javelins, ΣA, *a gem of excellent
design and exquisite execution*                     1

15 One, Wheel, *rev.* Taras to right, old style; Another, Warrior near his horse, standing to right, *rev.* Taras to left,
waves, &c.                                          2

16 One, Victory crowning the horse going to left, *rev.* Taras with
shield, spears and ΣOP, One, *rev.* Owl adjunct      2

17 Tarentum, didrachms as the following lots: one *obv.* figure
with cantharus seated to right; another with the figure
to left, both *rev.* Taras on dolphin to left, *rare and desirable*                                            2

18 Rider to left, ΞΕΝΟΚΡΑΤΗΣ., *rev.* Taras full-faced with
spear on dolphin to left, &c. *very valuable*        1

19 Others, varied and with ΞΕΝΟΚΡΑΤΗΣ.                3

20 Others (*ut videntur*) ΑΡΙΣΤΟΚΛΕΣ. *varied;* ΘΙΛΟΚΡΑΤΗΣ 4

21 Others, ΦΙΛΟΚΡΑΤΗΣ, dolphin, &c. *all varied*       5

22 Metapontium, fine bearded Ear of Wheat and MET., (old
style characters) *rev.* incuse                 *size* 8¼.   1

23 *Obv.* Female Head (Proserpine?) to right, in garland, *rev.*
MET. bearded wheat, and A. *excellent didrachm*      1

24 Posidonia, *obv.* ΠΟΣ. Neptune (archaic) to right, with
Chlamys, about to hurl his trident, *rev.* same incuse, but
ΓOM. in relief, *fine*                          *size* 8.   1

25 Posidonia, *obv.* Neptune to right, *rev.* Bull stepping to left,
varied didrachms (one with E. and Ħ.)                2

26 Sybaris, YM. Bull (symbolical of the great river Crathis) to left, head reverted, *rev.* incuse, *one fine, one oxidated, both desirable*        *size* 7.   2

27 Thurium, *very valuable small medallion, obv.* fine Head of Pallas to right, on helmet the monster Scylla and dogs, *rev.* Bull butting to right, ΘΟΥΡΙΩΝ, in exergum, sprig and ♨. *rare*        *size* 7.   1

28 Another, smaller, ΣΙ. behind helmet, *rev.* adjuncts ΝΙ. and sea serpent, *also valuable*        *size* 6.   1

29 Caulonia Apollo (Archaic) to right, stag, &c. *rev.* incuse, *a gem*        *size* 9.   1

30 Another, *equally desirable*        *size* 8½.   1

31 Crotona, *obv.* Tripod and Crab, *rev.* incuse, *obv.* diota near the tripod, *all in relief;* one, figure near tripod; one, *rev.* incuse flying Eagle, *very good didrachms*        3

32 Crotona, *obv.* Eagle to left, *rev.* Tripod between serpent coiled, and ear of wheat, *a fine valuable didrachm*        1

33 Rhegium, Tetradrachm, Lion's Head, *advers, rev.* senile Man seated to left        1

34 Tetradrachm, Messana type, *rev.* REϽINOW. backwards, hare to right, &c. *rare;* Drachm, *rev.* Bull's Head to right        2

35 Terina, Head of the Goddess Terina to left, *rev.* Nymph seated to left, *a scarce didrachm*        1

36 Agrigentum, Didrachm, *obv.* dumpy Eagle standing to left, *rev.* crab        1

37 Catana, *splendid and rare tetradrachm, obv.* laurelled full-faced Head of a female with abundant *" chevelure," rev.* fine quadriga to left, slender fish underneath, *highly valuable*        1

38 Catana, *obv.* Head of Apollo or female to right, *rev.* biga to right, *a rare tetradrachm*        1

39 Another, *nearly as good*        1

40 Another, and a Drachm, *obv.* Head to left between three fishes, *rev.* Quadriga to right, *fair and rare*        2

41 Gela, Tetradrachms, *rev.* slow Biga, one with Ionic column, starting or winning post; Didrachm, *rev.* Horseman to right        3

42 Heracleia, fine Tetradrachm, *obv.* female Head to right, *rev.* with Punic characters under quadriga to left, Victory above, caduceus in front of horses, *highly interesting and valuable; v.* Salinas    1

43 Another, no legend, *inferior ;* Himera, Cock to left, *rev.* the Agrigentine Crab, *didrachm*    2

44 Leontini, *obv.* Head of Apollo to right, *rev.* Lion's head to right, &c. *a very good tetradrachm*    1

45 Leontini, *obv.* and *rev.* as before, *finer*    1

46 Another, peculiar style of Lion's head, *rev.* slow Biga to right, *most desirable*    1

47 One, *obv.* Head to left, *rare, rev.* Lion's head to left, in circlet, &c. *highly preserved and interesting*    1

48 Zancles, Siciliæ, *the rare drachm,* Dolphin to left, and **DANKLE.** in a curve (the harbour), *rev.* Shell between thirteen squares, triangles, &c., *as Torremuzza,* xlv, 9, *fine and desirable*    1

49 Messana, antique style, 494 B.C. *obv.* Head of Lion, *adv. rev.* Head of Calf to left, around it **MESSENION.,** *a valuable tetradrachm*    1

50 Messana, *obv.* slow Biga to right, *rev.* fine Hare to right, dolphin beneath, *an excellent tetradrachm*    1

51 Messana, *obv.* Car drawn by only one Mule to right, *rev.* Fly beneath the " lepus timidus," both to right, *a rare tetradrachm ; obv.* Charioteer is seated on back of car, *rev.* Leveret    2

52 Messana, Biga to left, dolphins in exergum, *rev.* Head of Pan beneath the Hare, both to left, *a very valuable tetra-drachm*    1

53 Naxus, Tetradrachm, *obv.* Head of the bearded Indian Bacchus to right, *rev.* bearded jovial old Silenus naked, with tail, seated and looking to left, at his Kantharos, *a very valuable gem*    1

54 Naxus, Drachm, same type, *of much value*    1

55 Naxus, Obolus, Youthful Head (Apollo) to left, *rev.* slightly varied from the above, *fine and scarce*    1

56 Panormus, *Gold double stater,* struck by the Carthaginians, Head of Ceres to left, *rev.* Horse standing to right, above radiated globe with hooded snakes, the Mihir, *valuable* 1

146.11.6

*Pearson*   57 Panormus, Tetradrachm, with beardless Head of Hercules in lion's scalp to right, *rev.* Horses head to left, and palm tree with fruit, *fine*   1    *1 8*

*Rollin*   58 Segesta, Didrachms, varied with head of the Nymph Egesta, mother of its founder, *fair*   2    *1 7*

*Hopkins*   59 Selinus, Tetradrachm, *obv.* Apollo and Diana the tutelar Deities to left in biga (as on the basso-relievo of the frieze of the temple of Phigalia), *rev.* the river-god Selinus to left, sacrificing to Aesculapius, with patera and branch at a triangular altar, cock at its base, leaf of expanded selinum, and a bull on a pedestal, *very fine and rare, a valuable production of the fifth or sixth century* B.C. *as the Carthaginians destroyed this celebrated city* 400 B.C.   1    *10 5*

*Rollin*   60 Selinus, *obv.* Biga to right, with the above Deities, *rev.* very similar to last, *also of much merit*   1    *2 5*

*Hopkins*   61 Syracuse, Chariot to right, drawn by three horses, above ΣVPAQOΣION. (mark the Q for K, *rare*); *rev.* female Head to left, in quad. incus. archaic style, as the specimen in Brit. Mus. *a valuable tetradrachm*   1    *7 10*

*Lincoln*   62 One, *rev.* Biga, *very good style;* two others, *varied*   3    *3 10*

*Rollin*   63 One, *rev.* with "*chignon,*" *rev.* Biga to left; another, sea-serpent beneath biga to right, *well preserved*   2    *5 5*

*Pearson*   64 One, with the Meander ornament, &c. on cap of the Female to right; another with band or diadem and *chignon*   2    *2 2*

*Do.*   65 Philistis, placid, intellectual veiled head to left, of this Queen, *rev.* fast quadriga to left and E, *temp.* Hiero II, *a fine tridrachm*   1    *3 5*

*Lincoln*   66 Gelo, diademed Head to left, *rev.* Victory in slow Biga to right, ΣYPAK. (OΣIOI) BA. Φ. ΓΕΛΩΝΟΣ. *a fine rare didrachm*   1    *4 2*

*Grant*   67 Gelo, fine Drachm, *rev.* Eagle, E. BA., &c.   1    *1 2*

*Bunbury*   68 Abdera, early Tetradrachm, with Gryphon or Hippogriff to left, *rev.* quad. incus. *very heavy antient style*   1    *10*

*Rollin*   69 Aenus, *obv.* front Head of Mercury with petasus, *rev.* ANION. Goat standing to right, vine in front, *a valuable tetradrachm*   1    *5 10*

*Do.*   70 Another, with Head to right, *rev.* Antelope or Goat to right, shell, &c.   1    *5 12*

*206 15*

71 Maroneia, Horse to left, Wheel above, *rev.* **ΜΗΤΡΟΦΟΝ.**, Vine with grapes, in quad. *an excellent tetradrachm*    1

72 One, with trident's head beneath the Horse to left, *rev.* **ΕΠΙ. ΕΥΠΟΛΕΟΣ.**, Vine in incuse quad. *also desirable*  1

73 One, *rev.* **ΜΗΤΡΟΔΟΤΟ.**, *rare and fair*    1

74 Lysimachus, *aureus*, *obv.* rude portrait of Alexander the Great, with regal diadem and ram's horn, deified as young Jupiter Ammon (*vide* Sardonyx in French Collection), *rev.* Pallas, **ΔΙΟ. ΤΟ.**, ornated trident, &c. *rare and very fine*    1

75 Æ, Tetradrachm, regal Head to right, *rev.* Pallas, two complicated mon. and ornated trident    1

76 Another, Head of young Hercules, *rev.* Jupiter with his Eagle seated, forehalf of lion, 7 and pentagon, *fair*  1

77 Acanthus, Lion to right mounted on and seizing the bull, *rev.* no legend, quad. incus., *a very early fine tetradrachm, old style*    1

78 Macedonia, Tetradrachm, beautiful Head of Diana to right (quiver and bow behind), occupying the centre of an ornated Macedonic buckler, which covers the whole *obv.*, *rev.* wreath of oak, within it knotted club in centre between hand crowning with laurel, **LEG.** and **ΜΑΚΕΔΟΝΩΝ.** on right of the club and **MX.** mon., *a perfect and rare gem, of very high value*    1

79 Bisaltae of Thrace (King Mossäs), horse and man with spear near it, to right, *rev.* quad. and some letters, **a** Drachm ; Lete, 2, oval Didrachms, satyr urging a female, semi-nude, *rev.* irregular quadratum incusum, *one fine, a very valuable lot*    3

80 Orestäe, **ΩΡΗΞΙ(ΩΝ)** retrograde, centaur carrying off a woman, *very rare and in very fine condition*    1

81 Archelaus of Macedon, Tetradrachm, horseman with two javelins to left, *rev.* goat's head to right in square indented, *rather barbarous, but scarce*    1

82 Amyntas, bearded head of Hercules to right, *rev.* **AMYNTA.**, horse to right in sunk square, *a fine didrachm*    size 5. 1

83 Philip II, Æ, adjunct trident's head ; *this and the following staters or didrachms are all perfect gems and in high relief*    1

*Lincoln* 84 Philip II, adjunct a cantharus      1

*Castellani* 85 Adjunct ivy leaf      1

*Curt* 86 Alexander the Great, *N*, *rev.* Victory, with long vexillum and wreath, a long palm in front and two Punic letters, ΣI., &c., *a gem*      1

*Rollin* 87 Adjunct a coiled serpent, *rare*      1

*Lincoln* 88 *Tetradrachms.* Expressive Head of Hercules, skin of lion's head differently arranged, *rev.* adjuncts helmet, ΔA., scabellum (or *mon.* ΠO.) beneath throne, *valuable*      1

*Pearson* 89 Usual type, adjuncts, plustrum and Πo., torch, &c., ΦI. and BΣ., 3

*Read* 90 Adjuncts, bow, fore part of ram, MP. & H., slender dolphin and ro      4

*Lincoln* 91 Adjuncts, bee, caduceus, cornucopia, M. and ΛY.      4

*Pearson* 92 Adjuncts, all varied      4

*Do.* 93 Philip III (Aridaeus) ΦIΛIΠΠOY., Tetradrachm in high relief, *rev.* adjuncts, full-faced Head of Helios or of Apollo surrounded with rays under the eagle, KY. beneath throne, with back, *a gem*      1

*L.* 94 Antigonus Gonatas, usual Tetradrachm, *obv.* Pan, &c., *rev.* PALLAS-PUGNANS., adjuncts, helmet crested, MP., &c. (*mon.*)      1

*Curt* 95 Philip V, *obv.* head of the hero Perseus helmeted, harpé, &c., on the Macedonian shield, *rev.* club in wreath of oak, *mon.*, a small club in exergue, *a singularly beautiful tetradrachm, highly valuable and extremely rare*      1

*Young* 96 Dyrrhachium, splendid varied didrachms, with cow and calf, *rev.* the so-called Garden of Alcinoüs, of about 300 B.C., *all very valuable*      3

*Pearson* 97 Corcyra, *obv.* KOPKYPAI., fore part of cow to right, *rev.* garden between grapes, diota, K & I., *a valuable didrachm*      1

*Young* 98 Anactorium, Leucas, Thyracea, under Corinthian influence, *fair didrachms*      3

*Rollin* 99 Locri-Opuntii, Didrachm no doubt struck at Opus, *of admirable style, obv.* Head of Proserpine to left, *rev.* the warrior Ajax to right, with sword and shield, within it Pegasus, *very valuable*      1

100 Bœotia, shield, *rev.* Diota between BOIΩ. : another, with AMΦI., *desirable didrachms*   2

101 Thebes, Didrachm of very early fabric ; another, ΘE. and vase, ivy leaves above it   2

102 Thebes, *obv.* ΘE. and bearded head of Bacchus crowned with ivy, *rev.* buckler, *a fine valuable didrachm*   1

103 Athens, *obv.* very archaic head of Minerva to right, *rev.* owl with closed wings looking, full-faced, between olive sprig and AΘE.. *a valuable old (about 500 B.C.) tetra-drachm*   1

104 Athens, usual Tetradrachms   2

105 Others (*thinner*), *rev.* owl on amphora, names of magistrates, adjuncts, Pegasus, &c., varied, *all rather fine*   4

106 Aegina, Didrachm of extreme antiquity and of especial interest, *obv.* tortoise or sea turtle, *rev.* rude square with five irregular divisions, *very fine and valuable*   1

107 Aegina, Drachm, *rev.* NI., dolphins, five divisions ; Achæan League or Confederacy, 5, varied cities, *all fine*   6

108 Four others of the Achaican Foedus, likewise varied ; Corinth, 3, one very early, another with owlet and Θ., one with dolphins adjunct, *rev.* Pegasus with curled wings, *good didrachms*   7

109 Sicyon, *obv.* chimœra, wreath and ΣE., *rev.* N. or Σ., flying dove within wreath, *a good didrachm*   1

110 Elis, *obv.* eagle preying on hare to left on convex buckler, *rev.* F(A). a fulmen, *a rare didrachm of the Eleans*   1

111 Eagle with hare to right, *of fine style as is the rev.* FA. and winged thunderbolt in sunk square, *very valuable didrachm*   1

112 Another, eagle with serpent to left, *rev.* finely ornated thunderbolt, F(A). at bottom, *also valuable*   1

113 One, eagle's head to left, *rev.* FA. and a thunderbolt within a wreath, *also rare and fine*   1

114 Another, admirably designed head of stately Juno to right, with ΓΑΛΕΙΩΝ. on her tiara, *rev.* FA., eagle on pediment to right in a garland, *scarce and very valuable*   1

115 Argolis, Dolphins placed contrarywise, *rev.* irregularly indented. *didrachm of very early period*   1

116 Apollonia of Crete, *obv.* rude head to right, *rev.* tripod, *valuable and rare, as all Cretan medals are*    size 7.   1

117 Cnossus, Head of Juno to right (*nearly perfect, beautiful profile*), *rev.* Meandrean cross or maze, star in middle, *scarce and very valuable*    size 7.   1

118 Eleuthernœ, head to left, *rev.* xoanon of Hercules nudus, standing full faced, *rather poor, but very rare*    size 7.   1

119 Gortys, or Gortyna, *obv.* Europe, forlorn, seated on the sacred plane, said never to shed its leaves, *rev.* bull to right looking to left (as if stung by a fly) and fastened by its legs    size 7.   1

120 Phaestus, cow in wreath to left, *rev.* naked xoanon of Hercules standing, with club and bow, looking to right, long palm, serpent, lion's skin, &c.    size 7.   1

121 Phaestus, ox or cow, *rev.* a fine polypus    size 7.   1

122 Phalasarna, *obv.* female head to right, *rev.* ΠΑ., trident, rare    size 7.   1

123 Carystus Euboea, early Didrachm, *obv.* ΚΑΡΥΣ., cock with human head to right, *rev.* type of the Dyrrhachian Cow and its calf, *noticeable*    1

124 Naxos, early Bacchic Didrachm, Kantharus adorned with grapes, small Bust above    1

125 Mithradates VI, valuable Tetradrachm, *obv.* Head diademed of the famous King of Pontus (*as a portrait, scarcely excelled in the whole class of Greek coins*), *rev.* Pegasus feeding, ΗΣ., crescent with star, H. in exergum, *an extra fine gem, highly interesting*    1

126 Mithradates VI, another, Pegasus, stag, ΚΗΣ., &c., *also very valuable*    1

127 Ariarathes, *obv.* Head, *rev.* Pegasus drinking: lyre, *a rare tetradrachm*    1

128 Sinope, *obv.* Head of the nymph Sinope to left, *rev.* ΣΙΝΩ., eagle to left on a tunny fish, *a notched, but extra fine drachm*    1

129 Heraclea, Timotheus and Dionysius ruling together, *obv.* fine Head to left of a female Bacchante, *rev.* ΤΙΜΟΘΕΟΥ. ΔΙΟΝΥΣΙΟΥ., Hercules near trophy, club at base, &c., *of extreme rarity*    size 5.   1

130 Prusias II, probably, as the portrait, with wing to right, *Hopkins*
differs from some attributed to Prusias I, *rev.* Jupiter,
&c., *a rare and fine tetradrachm, more scarce than those
of the Nicomedi* 1

131 Nicomedes I, Tetradrachm, MPE., *mon.* and date, AΣP., *Bimbury*
*rare and valuable* 1

132 Nicomedes II, another, MYΩE., *mon.* and date, ⊥ПР (year *Dodgson*
188). *very good* 1

133 Nicomedes III, with ΘΔE., &c., *mon.* and date, ГOP., *extra fine*, 1 *Lincoln*

134 Cyricus, *N*, Di. Stater, *obv.* ram to left on tunny fish, *rev.* *Hopkins*
quad. inc., *irregularly shaped, very heavy and very finely
preserved* 1

135 Cyricus, *R*, *rev.* with ⊥ — BUCRANIUM., and tunny fish *Do.*
behind the lion's head to left size 6. 1

136 Philetairus (Attalus I), *obv.* portrait, narrow fillet, *rev.* A *Pearson*
on throne, bow behind and ivy or vine leaf near buckler
of Pallas, *fine tetradrachm, as are the next* 1

137 Eumenes II, laureated, *rev.* the monogram of EYMHNOΣ., *Do.*
adjunct Bee, bow and shield behind Pallas, *also fine and
scarce* 1

138 Another, varied 1 *Do.*

139 Attalus II, grapes, A., &c., *high relief* 1 *Rollin*

140 Attalus II, ivy leaf, A., &c., *a delicate tetradrachm* 1 *Pearson*

141 Uncertain Kings of Pergamus (quite different portraits), *Rollin*
*fair tetradrachms* 2

142 Scepsis, *obv.* ΣKHΨION., forepart of curled winged Sea *Do.*
Horse to right, as on coins of Lampsacus, *rev.* Palm-
tree, grapes, &c. in a dotted square, *extremely rare;
a perfect drachm* size 3½. 1

143 Ephesus, *obv.* fine head of Diana to right, *rev.* sacred Half *Bimbu*
Stag to right, but head looking to left, EΦ. across the
field, sacred bee and (*ut vid.*) EPMONAΣ.; another,
NIKIAΣ.; one, ГYPAI., *a very valuable lot* s. 5. 3

144 Smyrna, *tetradrachm*, *obv.* mural crowned head of Cybele
to right, *rev.* ΣMYPNAIΩN. EPMIППOΣ. ΣIПYΛOY.,
Lion to right, all in a coronet of oak-leaves, *well spread* *Lincoln*
*and valuable as few coins are more rare* s. 8¼. 1

145 Maussolus, *tetradrachm*, fine head of Apollo, laureate,
facing, *rev.* standing figure of the Carian Jupiter to right, *Rollin*
holding a two-headed axe and a long sceptre, *of very
great rarity, beauty and value* 1

485. 19. 6

Rollin 146 Pixodarus, *the didrachm, obv.* and *rev.* type as before, *also worthy of a good price*    1    5-

Pearson 147 Rhodus, *fine didrachm,* of about 500 B.C., *obv.* full-faced placid radiated head of Apollo as Helios, *rev.* Rose    1    1 15

Lincoln 148 Cameirvus Rhodi, leaf of the fig-tree, *rev.* indented, *a rare stater*    1    3 10

Pearson 149 Perekle-Lycia, *tridrachm, obv.* Lion's scalp or skin, *adv. rev.* with triskele (resembling a ring with hooks) and Lycian inscription (ΔF. &c.), *fine and valuable*    1    3 15

Lincoln 150 Lycia, *didrachm, obv.* forepart of Wild Boar to left, *rev.* rough indentation ; *Hemi-drachm,* Lion's scalp, *rev.* Triskele and numerous Lycian characters    2    1 1

Young 151 Aspendus, Wrestlers and ΛΦ., *rev.* Slinger and triquetra 1    1-

Dobson 152 Mallus, *obv.* Mercury and a female standing, *rev.* Pallas seated to left, *a fine rare didrachm*    1    3 5

Rollin 153 Nagidus, *rev.* Female seated to left, sacrificing at an altar, figure behind crowning her, *an elegant scarce didrachm* 1    10 15

Pearson 154 Cyprus or Cilicia, of uncertain Monarch, *obv.* Man to right, *rev.* Lion seizing on a stag to right, *a dumpy didrachm* 1    8

Collin 155 Tralles, Cistophorus of the Proconsul C. Pulcherius, *valuable*    1    1 15

Young 156 Tralles, usual Cistophorus, with TPA., small head of Helios to right, &c., *also rare*    1    13

Lumbury 157 Laodiceia, valuable Cistophorus, ΛΑΟ. and caduceus; over the quiver, between serpents, ΑΦΟΒΗΤΟΣ. ΦΙΝΤΙΠΟΥ., *a neat specimen*    1    3

Rollin 158 Cappadocia, *a most rare tetradrachm of Ariarathes IV, (sometimes erroneously given to the Vth and VIth), obv.* Portrait to right, *rev.* Pallas Victrix to left, &c., as *Mt.* IV, *and S.* VII, *pl.* 14, *and at page* 718, *v. also Northwick's Cat. lot* 1258, *of much value, seems to have* B *in exergue = year* 2    1    12

159 Cappadocian Drachms, with varied well executed portrait , &c.    5    1

534. 11. 6

# SECOND DAY'S SALE.

LOT

160 Seleucus I of Syria, *tetradrachm (as are the following 25 lots)*, *obv.* type of Alexander the Great, *rev.* Jupiter seated, with two *mons.*, *fine bold work and condition*   1

161 Seleucus I, *obv.* King's Head to right, in close helmet (with *mentonnieres*) mainly formed of skin of bull's head, with horn and ear, *rev.* Victory erecting trophy, radiated head at her feet, and two *mons.*, *of great rarity and value; authentic portrait, as all the next*   1

162 Antiochus I (ΣΩΤΗΡΟΣ.) Apollo seated   1

163 One, with ΒΑΣΙΛΕΩΣ. and two *mons.*   1

164 Seleucus II, *rev.* Apollo standing with arrow, leaning on a tripod ; two *mons.*, *extremely rare, and in beautiful condition ; some reverses are of feminine aspect*   1

165 Antiochus Hierax, Portrait, diademed and winged, *rev.* with two *mons.*, horse in exergum ; *also very scarce, and highly valuable*   1

166 Antiochus III (Magnus), *rev.* Owl on Apollo's right knee, *a gem, likewise in high relief*   1

167 One, *obv.* Border round the varied portrait, *rev. mon.* near the javelin   1

168 One, portrait more aged, *rev. mon.* AP. and HP., *a most desirable specimen*   1

169 Antiochus V (ΕΥΠΑΤΟΡΟΣ.), *obv.* his Portrait, *rev.* Jupiter seated, &c.   1

170 Demetrius I (with ΣΩΤΗΡΟΣ.), *obv.* bold Portrait, *rev.* Tyche seated, a winged syren supports the throne, two *mons.* ΞP beneath (year 160 of the Seleucian era = 152 B.C.)   1

171 One, date ΘNP and two *mons.*   1

172 Another, with two *mons.* and dated HNP   1

173 One *obv.* without the Soter, beautiful Portrait in fine garland, *rev. mon.* ΠΑ. in front of the seated female   1

174 Another, varied, *in middling condition*   1

175 Alexander I (Bala) struck at Tyre, *obv.* fine Portrait to right, *rev.* Eagle on prow of galley, *mon.* of Tyre on club, HP. *mon.* and date ΓΞP. (year 163), *very fine state* 1

176 One *rev.* with ΘΕΟΠΑΤΟΡΟΣ. ΕΥΕΡΓΕΤΟΥ., Jove with victoriola, ÇΙP. (163) and *mon.* in exergue, &c., *extremely fine* 1

177 Demetrius II (Nicator), *obv.* beardless Portrait, his earliest Tetradrachm, *rev.* seated Apollo, *mons.* and HΞP. (168), *rare* 1

178 One minted at Tyre, Eagle, ᴬₚₑ, &c., *very fine* 1

179 Another, a little different, *fine* 1

180 One *obv.* diademed bearded Portrait of the restored King, *rev.* Jupiter-Victor seated, and two *mon.*, *a gem* 1

181 Antiochus VI, fine young Portrait, radiated and diademed, *rev.* with all titles, Dioscuri on horseback, behind them ΤΡΥ., ΠΑΟ. *mon.*, date ΘΞP. (169) and ΣΤΑ., all within laurel wreath, *in very good preservation and extremely scarce and valuable* 1

182 Tryphon, Drachm, *obv.* Portrait of the former, *rev.* remarkable for the spiked Macedonian helmet, with ibex horn projecting in ront, *as on Tryphon's extremely rare tetradrachm, a valuable gem* 1

## TETRADRACHMS—*continued.*

183 Alexander II (Zebina), *rev.* Jupiter seated, two *mons.* 1

184 Antiochus VIII (Epiphanes), usual Portrait, *rev.* Jupiter naked supporting the star of day or prosperity, long sceptre, crescent above his head and the letter M under the star 1

185 Cleopatra and Antiochus VIII (Autonomous Tetradrachm), *obv.* united diademed deified Heads to right, stars above, *rev.* ΤΡΙΠΟΛΙΤΩΝ. &c., Abundance to left, Γ. ΗΙ. Θ. and star, *rare, minted at Tripolis* 1

186 Antiochus IX (Philopator) with short beard, *rev.* Minerva-Victrix to left, HP. *mon.* and a Phœnician character (or rough cornucopia) all in wreath, *rare, very fine rev* 1

187 Seleucus VI (Epiphanes), Jupiter Victor seated, *very rare and fair* 1

188 Antiochus X (Eusebes Philopator), Jupiter seated, *in good state and extremely scarce*  1

189 Antiochus XI (Epiphanes), Zeus seated holding Nike, PEA. reading downwards, *fine*  1

190 Tigranes, regal expressive Bust with strange Oriental (Armenian) head-dress, *rev.* Antioch on rock Silpius, with mural crown and palm branch, the river Orontes personified at her feet, &c., as on gems, &c. after Euty-chides of Sicyon, all within wreath, *a rare and fine tetra-drachm*  1

191 Seleuccia, Autonomous Tetradrachm of fair style, *obv.* veiled turreted Bust to right, *rev.* long legend and a thunderbolt on the throne of Jupiter, dated AI. (year 10th of the autonomy of the City), *fine and scarce*  1

192 Tyre, usual Tetradrachms of a Tyrian monarch or of the God Hercules, *rev.* Eagle on prow, LK. Z.B.; another, with BZ. and *mon.*, *both desirable*  2

193 Aradus, 2, Drachms, Bee, *rev.* Stag  2

194 Judaea. Shekel of the Prince High Priest Jaddæus, usual types and old Hebrew legends, *obv.* Aaron's Rod that budded, *rev.* Chalice or pot of manna with two handles, above ש״ו = 2nd year of Israel's freedom, *fine and valuable, first mentioned in Genesis XXIV*  1

195 Half Shekel, ש״ו = 3rd year, *the rarest date, also of great merit and value*  1

196 San'ā (in Arabia), Æ, *obv.* Head to right in wreath, *rev.* Owl on amphora, &c., *cf. Schlumberger, " Tresor de Sana, 1880," as pl. 1, n.* 15, 17, 20 *(slightly different), rare and fine*  size 7.  4

197 San'ā, Æ, others, *v. pl. 1, n.* 14, 16, 20 *(three varied)*  sizes 6-7.  5

198 San'ā, Æ, *v. pl. 2, n.* 29, 34, 36; one *obv.* Head to left, *rev.* very like n. 29 ; two others, *rather blurred*  6

199 AV, Double Daric or Di-Stater of Darius-Hystaspi, King to right on one knee, with bow and arrow, of about 521-485 B.C., *very fine, and certainly authentic*  1

200 Daric or Stater, *very good*

201 Æ, Persian Didrachm, *obv.* Artaxerses II, King  or Satrap on sea-horse to right, *rev.* Owl, full-faced, flail, &c., *fine* 1

202 Another, *less perfect;* one *obv.* bearded King's Head to right, *rev.* Galley and twelve rowers, *fine* 2

203 Same type, 2 ; Hemi-drachms ; two others have *rev.* Fire-altar, Magi, &c., *well preserved* 5

204 Arsaces V of Parthia, Drachm, fine Bust to left, *rev.* King with bow, seated to right, *a gem* 1

205 Valarsaces, the brother of the Parthian King Arsaces VI, *obv.* bearded Head to left, *rev.* King seated to right, *a very rare, fine and valuable tetradrachm, v. Prokesch-Osten* 1

206 Parthian Tetradrachms of Arsaces XX (ENT., year 355), XXIV, and another Monarch, *rare and fine for the period* 3

207 Sassanidee, Æ, 5, of different Kings ; one Æ, also *rev.* Altar, *all fine* 6

208 Bactriana, 2, *obv.* Ox, *rev.* Elephant, *square;* Drachms and three ½ Drachms, *fine* 5

209 Indo Scythian, varied Aurei of Kanerki and Hoerki, *fine and rare* 2

210 Cilicia (Autonomous, about 450 B.C.), *N*, Lion seizing stag to right, *rev.* Hercules to right, uncertain regal, *fine and of high numismatic interest* size 2. 1

211 Alexander the Great, or Alexander Aegus or junior, son of Alexander the Great and Roxana, *obv.* Head with elephant head dress, *rev.* Jupiter type, with eagle, fulmen, ΔΦH. or HΦ. *mon.* beneath throne, *v. Cat. of the Huber Collection, 1862, at lot 942, &c., a complete, extra rare and valuable tetradrachm* 1

212 Another, *rev.* Pallas to right hurling a spear, ΔΦ. *mon.* (Daphne), branch, eagle, &c., *r. type of Antigonus Gonatas, of greatest beauty* 1

213 Another, with A. EV., *also of much value* 1

214 Another, three *mon.*, eagle, &c., *highly valuable and fine, though the proboscis and tusks are off the tetradrachm* 1

*⁎* All found in Egypt.

215 Ptolemæus I (Soter), *N*, Head to right, *rev.* Quadriga of Elephants to left, two *mon.*, *v. Pinder and Friedlander,* 1851, *pl.* VIII, *n.* 10, *extra rare*                         1

216 *R*, Tetradrachm, *rev.* Eagle to left and Σ I. (Sidon), *fine*  1

217 *N.*  Ptolemæus I and II (Philadelphus), *rev.* Arsinoe and Berenice, ΘΕΩΝ. and ΑΔΕΛΦΩΝ., buckler behind, *a valuable di-stater or gold tetradrachm*          *size* 6.  1

218 Arsinoe, *N*, veiled diademed Bust of the beautiful Queen, with lotus and K, *rev.* two Cornucopiæ united by a flowing diadem, with grapes and other fruit, *a valuable gem*                              *size* 8.  1

219 *R*, Medallion, *obv.* veiled Portrait, *rev.* Cornucopia with fasciæ flowing, &c., as on the gold                        1

220 Another, *also of exquisite design, equally rare and good*   1

221 Ptolemæus VIII, Tetradrachm, Eagle between LA. and ΠΑ., *extremely beautiful*                               1

222 Cyrene, *N*, ΚΥΡΑΝΑΙΩΝ., Jupiter with long sceptre standing to right, *rev.* Victory in slow quadriga to left                                       *size* 4½.  1

223 *N*, Jupiter seated to right, *rev.* fast victorious Quadriga to left, and traces of ΚΥΡΑΝΑΙΩΝ. in exergum   *size* 4.  1

224 *N*, Jupiter seated to left, eagle or dove and traces of letters, *rev.* Quadriga in quick motion to left, and legend on scroll beneath                         *size* 4.  1

225 Numidia (Micipsa), Didrachm; Hiempsal II, 2, Drachms, *rev.* Horse, *fine*                                    3

## IMPERIAL ROMAN GOLD COINS.

### CHIEFLY IN PERFECT CONDITION.

226 Julius Cæsar, *obv.* laureated Head, &c. on his being created Perpetual Dictator in 710, assassinated the same year (B.C 44), *rev.* bare head of Julius Octavius, afterwards called Augustus, *a rare, valuable gem  as are many of the following* 140 *gold coins*                       1

227 Augustus, *rev.* MAR. VLT., circular Temple of Mars the Avenger, and the standards recovered from the Parthians after 33 years                               1

*Lincoln* 228 *Rev.* AVGVSTVS., the Capricorn, Constellation under the influence of which he was born 1

*Verity* 229 Tiberius, *rev.* Livia (the devoted) seated to right, *fine* 1

*Curt* 230 Antonia, *obv.* beautiful Portrait to left, as Ceres, *rev.* Constancy standing, struck to her memory by Claudius, *a desideratum for any cabinet, exquisite in expression, workmanship and preservation* 1

*Lincoln* 231 Claudius, *rev.* triumphal Thensa or quadriga, &c. *in bold relief* 1

*Do.* 232 *Rev.* PACI. AVGVSTAE., Nemesis, with attributes, &c., as on gems, *fine delicate work* 1

*Do.* 233 Nero, *rev.* Claudius and Agrippina junior standing, *of high state of art* 1

*Do.* 234 Galba, *obv.* bare Head, *rev.* oaken Garland (or Corona civica) and S.P.Q.R. OB. C. S., *of known merit* 1

*Baker* 235 Galba, *obv.* laureate Bust, *rev.* IMP.CAES. TRAIAN. &c., Liberty standing to left, *a valuable rare restoration by the Emperor Trajan* 1

*Rollin* 236 Otho, *obv.* Head, with wig, to right, *rev.* SECVRITAS. P. R., Female with garland and long wand, *fine and valuable likewise, on account of his ephemeral reign* 1

*Do.* 237 Vitellius, *rev.* Concord seated, *fine, and more rare than generally supposed* 1

*Lincoln* 238 Vespasian, *rev.* Peace or Nemesis, very similar to an Aureus of Claudius (*v. lot* 232), *fine* 1

*Do.* 239 Titus, *rev.* TR. P. VIIII. IMP. XV. &c., fine Trophy, *v. Bede, Gibbon and Wiczay, a gem* 1

*Mason* 240 *Rev.* COS. V., Rome sitting on shields between eagles flying, and Remus and Romulus suckled by the wolf, *v. Romilia gens, in* BORGHESI, *of much merit and value* 1

*Lincoln* 241 Domitian, fine high-relief Bust of Pallas, Goddess of Arts, &c., to left, *a perfect gem* 1

*Newbury* 242 *Rev.* Germany reclining on the shield of her country, &c., *also highly preserved* 1

*Lincoln* 243 *Rev.* COS. IIII., Cornucopia, *fine* 1

*Do.* 244 *Rev.* Minerva on prow, to right, *fine* 1

*Robert* 245 *Rev.* Minerva on prow, *slightly different* 1

*Pratt* 246 *Rev.* Minerva, varied, *also desirable* 1

D

247 Nerva, *rev.* CONCORDIA. EXERCITVVM., Hands joined, *very fine and scarce, his aurei all bear high prices* 1

248 Trajan, *rev.* PARTHICO. &c., Head of the Sun, *quite a gem, in perfect condition* 1

249 *Rev.* FORVM. TRAIANI., Apollodorus' greatest work, completed A.D. 114 1

250 *Rev.* three Military Ensigns 1

251 Plotina, *rev.* Bust of Trajan, in memory of his father, and struck by Hadrian, A.D. 118, *fine, and extra rare* 1

252 *Rev.* Empress as Vesta, with palladium and long sceptre, *valuable* 1

253 Trajan the Father, *rev.* laureate Bust of the Emperor Trajan, *also scarce and valuable* 1

254 Trajan, *rev.* fine Bust of Hadrian 1

255 Matidia, *rev.* Empress as Charity, caressing two children, *a rare type and valuable* 1

256 Hadrian, *rev.* the rare ADVENTVI. AVG. ITALIAE. type, *a truly fine and striking historic record* 1

257 *Rev.* DISCIPLINA. AVG., Emperor to right, followed by three soldiers, *rare and highly desirable* 1

258 *Rev.* ORIENS. DIVI. NER. REP. P. M. TR. P. COS., Head of the Sun, *the rarest variety of legend of this type* 1

259 *Rev.* She-wolf and the famed twins, as on gems, *very fine* 1

260 *Rev.* Hadrian's equestrian Monument to right, *fine* 1

261 *Rev.* GENIO. P. R., the Roman Genius sacrificing at an altaret, to left 1

262 *Rev.* Jupiter, *a fine aureus* 1

263 *Rev.* Hope, *very fine* 1

264 Sabina, *obv.* Bust, with the Matidian style head-dress, *rev.* no legend, Empress as Vesta, seated, with palladium and long sceptre, *of great value* 1

265 *Obv.* Bust, varied, *rev.* VESTA., type as before 1

266 *Obv.* Bust, also different, *rev.* as the last 1

267 Aelius, splendid noble Bust to right, *rev.* PIETAS. TRIB. &c., veiled Figure sacrificing to right, opposite a flaming altar 1

268 Antoninus Pius, high-relief Bust to right, *rev.* LIB. V. COS. IIII., Female (or Liberality) to left. with tessera and cornucopia, *a gem* 1

*464 - - -*

| | | | | |
|---|---|---|---|---|
| *Lincoln* | 269 | Antoninus Pius, *rev.* VOTA. &c., Emperor sacrificing to left, *fine*    1 | 3 | 3 |
| *Rollin* | 270 | *Rev.* TR. &c., Emperor performing sacrifice to right, *fine* 1 | 2 | 8 |
| *Lincoln* | 271 | *Rev.* PAX. &c., Peace to left, *high relief*    1 | 2 | 6 |
| *Verity* | 272 | *Rev.* COS. IIII., Equity, with cornucopia and scales, *also fine, as are the following*    1 | 2 | 4 |
| *Rollin* | 273 | *Rev.* COS. IIII., Antoninus to left    1 | 2 | 2 |
| *Verity* | 274 | *Rev.* TR. POT. XIX. COS. IIII., Emperor to left    1 | 2 | .. |
| *Rollin* | 275 | Faustina the Elder, *rev.* CERES.    1 | 3 | 18 |
| *Lincoln* | 276 | Aurelius, *obv.* youthful bare Head to right, *rev.* the interesting HILARITAS. type, *a gem, as are the three next ; the best period of Roman art was that between the reigns of Augustus and this Emperor*    1 | 5 | 15 |
| *Rollin* | 277 | *Rev.* CONCORDIAE, &c., Aurelius and Verus    1 | 3 | 10 |
| *Do.* | 278 | *Rev.* Victory to right, resting a round buckler, inscribed VIC. AVG., against palm tree, *also most desirable*    1 | 3 | 8 |
| *Do.* | 279 | *Rev.* SALVTI. AVGVSTOR. TR. P. XVI. COS. III., Hygeia to left    1 | 3 | 12 |
| *Do.* | 280 | *Rev.* as the former, but TR. P. XVII.    1 | 4 | 8 |
| *Do.* | 281 | Faustina the Younger, with " Chignon," *rev.* SALVTI. AVGVSTAE., the renowned beautiful Empress, as the Goddess of Health, seated to left    1 | 3 | 6 |
| *Do.* | 282 | Verus, fine expressive Bust, like those Busts found at Rome in 1806, *rev.* Emperor galloping, with spear levelled at a prostrate foe, as on gems, &c.    1 | 6 | 10 |
| *Do.* | 283 | *Rev.* ARMEN. &c., disconsolate Captive, trophy, &c., *also very interesting*    1 | 4 | 10 |
| *Lincoln* | 284 | *Rev.* Victory to left, *likewise a perfect exemplar*    1 | 4 | 4 |
| *Rollin* | 285 | *Rev.* Fortune seated to left, COS. II.    1 | 5 | |
| *Lincoln* | 286 | *Rev.* PROFECTIO. &c., equestrian Imperial Figure, *also rare*    1 | 4 | 15 |
| *Rollin* | 287 | Lucilla, *rev.* Empress as Venus, *a gem*    1 | 5 | 2 6 |
| *Lincoln* | 288 | *Rev.* the rare PIETAS. type, Empress in pietistic robes, &c. 1 | 2 | 2 |
| *Do.* | 289 | *Rev.* VOTA. PVBLICA,, within garland    1 | 4 | 2 6 |
| *Hopkins* | 290 | Crispina, *obv. cf.* her Bust in our British Museum, *rev.* Empress as Venus Felix, seated, *valuable*    1 | 1 | 15 |
| *Rollin* | 291 | Domna, *obv.* JVLIA. DOMNA. AVG., Bust to right, *rev.* VENERI. VICTR., Empress as the Cyprian Goddess, *highly valuable*    1 | 6 | 2 6 |

*53/ - - 6*

292 Elagabalus, *obv.* IMP., &c., *rev.* sun to left, with whip, star in field (*as almost always seen on his coins, never on Caracalla's, besides he is generally styled "Imp," and Caracalla but very seldom*), *cf. Lampridius, a valuable aureus*   1

293 Alexander Severus, Aureus, *as usual, rev.* Emperor with lance and globe to left (*as a rare quinarius*), *of much rarity*   1

294 *Rev.* P.M. TR. P. COS. P.P., Health seated   1

295 *Rev.* P.M. TR. P. II. COS. P.P., the Goddess of Hygiene, as before   1

296 Gordian III, *rev.* Providence to left, *rather scarce*   1

297 *Rev.* Emperor as Hercules, standing, *in* A.D. 242, *aged* 21, *he distinguished himself in a battle against Sapor*   1

298 Otacilia, *obv.* Bust of the Christian Empress, *rev.* the CONCORDIA. AVGG. type, *very valuable*   1

299 Trajan Decius, *rev.* Abundance to right, *rare*   1

300 *Rev.* equestrian statue of Decius, *rare*   1

301 Galerius Maximian, *rev.* SOLI. INVICTO. and NE. mon., SMN , in exergum, Emperor as Helios, *a rare specimen* 1

302 Constantine the Great, *rev.* the PRINCIPI. JVVENTVTIS. type of Constantine in military habit, to right, with spear and globe, P.TR. as exergue, *fine and valuable* size 3½.   1

303 *Rev.* VIRTVS. EXERCITVS. GALL. and PTR., Mars with trophy and spear moving to right, *also fine and rare* size 3¼.   1

304 Constans II, *rev.* VICTORIA. AVGVSTORVM. SMAN., Victory seated on armour, inscribing VOT. XXX. on a round shield supported by a winged boy   ½ *sol d'or*, size 2½.   1

305 Magnentius, Sol d'Or, *rev.* VICT. CAES. (*in general* AVG.) LIB. ROM. ORB., Victory and female, trophy between them, *varied from Cohen's No.* 141, *fair preservation*   1

306 Decentius, *rev.* VICTORIA. AVG. LIB. ROMANOR., TR. in exergue, two figures supporting a trophy   1

307 Constantius Gallus, *rev.* GLORIA. REIPVBLICAE. and VOT. V. MVLT. X., in exergue TES., *a gem*   1

308 Julian II the Apostate, *rev.* the VIRTVS. EXERCITVS. ROMANORVM. type, SIRM. and wreath as exergue   1

*Archer* 309 Julian II, the Apostate, bearded, *rev.* variety of the last type, *finer* 1

*Rollin* 310 Jovian, *rev.* the SECVRITAS. REIPVBLICAE. type and ANTI. 1

*Curt* 311 *Rev.* varied, ANT. △. 1

*Pearson* 312 Valentinian I (or III, *who first recognised the Pope as head of the Church*), fine Bust to left, *rev.* SALVS. REIP., Emperor with victoriola, labarum with *mon.* of our Saviour (*first placed on his banners and coins by Constantine*), captive, star, SMSIS. and palm beneath, *a gem* 1

*Rollin* 313 Gratian, *rev.* Emperor and Valentinian junior, exergue TESOB., *very fine* 1

*Prankerd* 314 Arcadius, *rev.* Emperor with labarum, Victory, captive and S.M., *fine* 1

*Jenkinson* 315 Honorius, *rev.* VICTORIA. AVGGG., Emperor, with staff surmounted by the *mon.* of Christ, standing on a panther (?), R.V. COB. in exergue 1

*Prankerd* 316 Theodosius Junior (II), *rev.* VOT. XXX. MVLT. XXXX., star, CONOB., &c., Solidus, *rev.* Victory seated to right; ½ Solidus, *the latest Roman coins found in England, v. Gibbon* xxxiv, *both fine* 2

*Rollin* 317 Eudoxia (the Poetess), *rev.* cross in garland, CONOB. as exergue, *a rare fine quinarius* 1

*Do.* 318 Johannes the Usurper, Aureus, *rev.* the rebel standing on a captive to right, COMOB. beneath, R.V. in field, *rare* (*valued abroad at £12*), *in very fair state though slightly holed* 1

*Prankerd* 319 Libius Severus (III), *rev.* VICTORIA. AVGGG. R.A., &c., Emperor with long cross, &c., *pale gold, a valuable aureus* 1

*Rollin* 320 Anthemius, *rev.* SALVS. REIPVBLICAE., Emperor and Leo standing full-faced, with spears, M.D. and in exergue COMOB., *a desirable bezant* 1

*Do.* 321 Quinarius, *rev.* cross in wreath, *also rare* 1

*Hopkins* 322 Glycerius, Quinarius, *rev.* cross as the former, *very scarce and fine* 1

*Lincoln* 323 Julius Nepos, Aureus, *rev.* VICTORIA. AVGGG. R.V. and COMOB., *rare and fine* 1

*Rollin* 324 Quinarius, *rev.* cross in wreath, *valuable* 1